The Big Parade

by Arlène Elizabeth Casimir • illustrated by Helen Flook

Lucy Calkins and Michael Rae-Grant, Series Editors

LETTER-SOUND CORRESPONDENCES

m, t, a, n, s, ss, p, i, d, g, o, c, k, ck, r, u, h, b, e, f, ff, l, ll, j, v, w, y, qu, -e

HIGH-FREQUENCY WORDS

is, like, see, the, no, so, of, says, go, to, for, look, was, you, she

The Big Parade
Author: Arlène Elizabeth Casimir
Series Editors: Lucy Calkins and Michael Rae-Grant

Heinemann
145 Maplewood Avenue, Suite 300
Portsmouth, NH 03801
www.heinemann.com

Cataloging-in-Publication data is on file with the Library of Congress.

ISBN-13: 978-0-325-13830-5

Design and Production: Dinardo Design LLC, Carole Berg, and Rebecca Anderson

Editors: Anna Cockerille and Jennifer McKenna

Illustrations: Helen Flook

Photographs: p. 32 (food truck) © Carolyne Parent/Shutterstock; inside back cover (boy pointing) © Khosro/Shutterstock; inside back cover (girl in rain) © A3pfamily/Shutterstock.

Manufacturing: Gerard Clancy

Printed in Dongguan, China
4 5 6 7 8 9 10 TP 28 27 26 25 24 23
April 2023 Printing / PO# 4500868396

Contents

Meet...

Lalin   Liv   Bel

Mom   Dad

The Best Spot

"The parade! The parade!"
says Lalin.

"I will look for a spot!"
yells Liv.

She runs off
to pick the best spot.

Mom and Dad set up camp.

Mom asks Bel to help.

But Bel just sits and pops gum.

"I can help!" Lalin says.

Mom and Dad grin.

Lalin sets up a jug
and a stack of cups.

"The parade will be fun!"
says Lalin.

"It will be HOT," says Bel.

"Well, we did get the best spot!"
says Liv.

"But it is not the best spot
for me," says Lalin.
"I can not see!"

Dad lifts Lalin up.

"Look!" says Lalin.
"I got the BEST spot...
on top of Dad!"

2

The Red Costume

The parade kicks off!

Bel jams, Liv hums,

and Lalin claps.

Mom and Dad tap, tap, tap.

"Look at the red costume!"

Lalin yells.

"It looks like a big fan!"

"Dad, let me off," says Lalin.

"So I can be in the parade!"

Lalin slips past so she can see...

…the red costume!

Look at him spin!

And look!

Lalin is in the parade!

"Look at the kid
in the hat!" Liv says.
"It is Lalin!"

Lalin gets back to
Mom and Dad.

"I was in the parade!"

Lalin says.

"Did you see?"

3

The Big Parade

We can go to the big parade.

It is fun!

Grab a spot to sit

so we can see it go past.

We can see a big band
of drums.

We can see flags flap.

We can see kids spin.

And look!

We can see a man

on top of a big truck.

He says, "Step, step, step!
Let's go!"

The sun will be hot,

so we can stop

and get a snack.

Run, run, run!

Let's get back to the parade.

Be quick!

So we will not miss it!

THE WEST INDIAN AMERICAN DAY PARADE

Every year in New York City, there's a famous parade called the *West Indian American Day Parade*. Millions of people march down the street to show that they're proud to be from Caribbean countries like Haiti, Jamaica, and Trinidad and Tobago.

Some of the yummiest food in New York City comes from food trucks.

At the parade, you will see colorful costumes covered with sparkles and feathers. You will hear music from the Caribbean, like soca, Kompa, and calypso. You will hear instruments like steel drums. You can sway your hips and move your feet to the rhythm!

If you're hungry, you can stop at a food truck. A *food truck* is like a restaurant on wheels. You can walk right up to the window and order foods like jerk chicken, roti, and coconut bread. Yum!

Talk about...

Ask your reader some questions like...

- What happened in this book?
- Turn to page 10. Why wasn't this a good spot for Lalin?

- How do you think Lalin felt when she was in the parade? Why?
- Would you want to go to a big parade? Why or why not?